The
FULFILLMENT

The
FULFILLMENT

Jesus and the Old Testament

TIMOTHY C. TENNENT

Printed in the United States of America

Paperback ISBN: 978-1-62824-242-3
Mobi ISBN: 978-1-62824-243-0
ePub ISBN: 978-1-62824-244-7
uPDF ISBN: 978-1-62824-245-4

Library of Congress Control Number: 2015955420

Cover design by Nikabrik Design
Page layout by PerfecType

SEEDBED PUBLISHING
Franklin, Tennessee
Seedbed.com
SOW FOR A GREAT AWAKENING

In memory of Bob Craine,
who was passionate about bridging the gap
between the marketplace and the church

Contents

The
FULFILLMENT

INTRODUCTION

Adam, Abraham, Moses, David, and the Suffering Servant

The Old Testament is both familiar and strange to many Christians. On one hand, the Old Testament contains some of the most familiar stories known to us. Many of us cannot remember a time when we didn't know the story of Jonah being swallowed up by a great fish or young David slaying the giant Goliath. What is more comforting or assuring than hearing the familiar strains of Psalm 23 at a time of difficulty or loss? On the other hand, the Old Testament can be intimidating and difficult to understand. Some parts of the Old Testament contain long genealogical lists that are tedious, and we wonder why they were included in the Bible. Others contain strange laws, and we wonder if they still apply to us today.

In the early part of my ministry, I pastored a small church in the mountains of north Georgia. Many of my parishioners were hardworking farmers. Their work ethic and godliness continue to inspire me to this day. However, they didn't have a lot of free time for reading or serious academic study of the Bible. As a pastor, I needed to find a way to help them understand the importance of the Old Testament. I felt that this was important for two reasons. First, the Old Testament is part of God's Word. All Scripture is inspired by God and has been given to us for our instruction (2 Tim. 3:16). Second, I realized early on that it is impossible to truly understand the New Testament without a sufficient grounding in the Old Testament. The entire New Testament is found in seed form in the Old Testament. All of the earliest Christians were Jews, and they fully understood that everything they encountered in Jesus Christ was fulfilling promises and prophecies that had been given to them in the Old Testament. To lack a basic knowledge of the Old Testament is a great hindrance to fully understanding Jesus Christ and how He fulfills various ideals and expectations present in the Old Testament.

After much reflection I realized that there was a relatively simple way to help Christians begin their fruitful relationship with the Old Testament. This is just a beginning, but it is an important first step. The key is to introduce Christians to a few important figures in the Old Testament and how they prepare us for fully understanding the New Testament gospel. But, again, where do we start? The Old Testament is filled with hundreds of people, such as Noah, Deborah, Balaam, Samson, Ruth, Elijah, and Isaiah, to name just a few. However, a careful read of the Old Testament, along with an examination of what Old Testament passages are referred to most often in the New Testament, reveals the particular importance of four key figures. There are four people who are of such immense importance that every Christian must know these figures and how we relate to them. To not understand these four is to lose a major aspect of who Jesus is. The New Testament extensively uses these four figures to explain the gospel and to fully reveal to us the importance of our Lord Jesus Christ. I have found that if a Christian knows these four figures and why they are so important to our understanding of the Christian gospel and of Jesus Christ, then the entire Old Testament becomes more accessible and more fully appreciated.

Who are these four people? *Adam, Abraham, Moses, and David.* It is these figures who open up to us vast parts of the Old Testament as well as the full significance of Jesus Christ. The devotionals that follow focus on these four figures and how each of them is fulfilled in some way through the ministry of Jesus Christ.

After these devotionals explore the four key figures, I have included (as the Old Testament does) a fifth, surprise figure. This fifth figure is one that is in the background of the Old Testament and is not really embodied in any one historical person, like Adam, Abraham, Moses, or David. This fifth figure is known as the Suffering Servant. The Suffering Servant is embodied in the experience of Israel as a whole. Israel experiences great suffering, and the prophets anticipate the coming of One who will bring redemption and healing through suffering. Once the earliest Christians received the full revelation of Jesus Christ, including His going to the cross, then they came to understand that Jesus not only fulfills ideals embodied in Adam, Abraham, Moses, and David, but also fulfills expectations regarding this future Suffering Servant that is prophesied about in the Old Testament.

I hope as you read and meditate on these devotionals, you will come to appreciate the Old Testament more fully. Even more, I pray that you will see with even greater clarity the full power and revelation of Jesus Christ.

CHAPTER 1

Adam: The Fall

Genesis 1:1—3:24

The first of our essential Old Testament figures is Adam, the head of the human race. His story is where we all start, and in his story we find our own. As we read the creation account of Genesis 1, we learn about the nature of humanity and the special qualities and responsibilities with which God endowed us. First, the creation of man and woman comes at the apex of God's work. All of creation culminates in the making of man and woman. Second, we are given dominion and stewardship over the whole of creation. God commands us to rule over the three realms He has created: the realms of light/darkness, water/sky, and earth/land. We are to be fruitful and multiply, to fill the earth, and to subdue it. Third, unlike the rest of creation, we are created in the image of God. Notice that the rest of creation emerges from God's spoken word, *ex nihilo*, meaning "out of nothing." God creates man, however, by shaping him from the dust of the earth and then breathing into him the breath of life. The word for breath, or wind, in the Old Testament is the same word for Spirit—*ruah*—so in the breath of God, the spirit of God was given to us. Animals have bodies, minds, and wills, but only we have spirits, which makes us distinct from all of creation. The entire created order was created for our enjoyment, for us to practice the dominion of God.

Created in the Image of God

What does it mean to say that we are created in the image of God? It does not refer to any physical resemblance with God because God, in His essence, is spirit, and therefore noncorporeal. No, the image of God means resemblance to Him in three other ways. First, it means that we are endowed with moral responsibility. We are able to obey the commands of God and are morally accountable for our actions. Second, the image of God means that we have the capacity for relationship with Him. We can know Him and be in fellowship and in communication with Him. Third, it means that we have representative capacity to act as His regents on the earth, stewarding and extending His dominion. As bearers of God's image, Adam and Eve possessed moral, relational, and representative capacity and were fully endowed with God's holiness and righteousness.

God created man and woman in His own image and placed them in the garden of Eden to be holy and to live in an ever-deepening relationship with Him. Everything they needed was provided in the garden. Genesis 2:15 says that the garden was given for them to *work* in, demonstrating that work is integral to God's plan for us and not just the result of human fallenness. Without the presence of sin, work is fulfilling and deeply satisfying. Even in eternity we will have meaningful work. God also provided *food* in this fruitful garden nestled between four lush rivers. Everything that was needed for sustenance and enjoyment was there. In the middle of the garden was a tree known as the Tree of the Knowledge of Good and Evil. This tree was an acknowledgment of what had already occurred before the creation of humanity. God had created an earlier order of angels, but some had rebelled and fallen and become agents of evil. By placing the Tree of the Knowledge of Good and Evil in the garden, God is, in effect, acknowledging that this reality exists, that Satan has been cast down and will tempt us, but warning us not to go there. It is not some arbitrary command or petty regulation; it is a danger sign, warning us that Satan is in the world and will try to win us over, but we must not join him in his rebellion.

Sin Breaks the Love Relationship with God

When Eve encounters Satan at the tree, Satan begins the same way that he begins today: by raising questions about God's word. The serpent asks, "Did God *really* say, 'You must not eat from any tree in the garden'?" (3:1, emphasis mine), misquoting God's words that they could eat from any tree of the garden except one (2:16–17). Choices are vital if we have a doctrine of holiness, not just innocence. Holiness must be confirmed by real acts of obedience in the presence of real choices. A machine can work flawlessly, but it can never be holy, because that involves capacities that machines do not have. You cannot have a relationship with a machine, because a machine has no choice in the relationship. You can force them to serve you, but they have no capacity to choose to obey or choose to love. Without choice, there is no love, no real relationship, no genuine holiness.

In Satan's rebellion, one-third of the angels disobeyed, but that confirmed the other two-thirds into a higher state of holiness, a higher confirmation of their choice to love. God turned even the evil of the rebellious into greater glory for the obedient. In the same way, choices become an opportunity to confirm one's holiness in a freewill act of choice. God placed the Tree of the Knowledge of Good and Evil in the garden because it provided an opportunity to confirm Adam and Eve's holiness through which they would live forever in a positive love relationship with God. Adam and

Eve, however, broke this love relationship by a willing act of disobedience, an assertion of their own wills against God. Satan offered Eve the sacrament of evil, and she partook. It functioned in the same way as our sacraments serve today; just as ordinary bread is endowed with sacred purpose and significance, so this ordinary fruit was endowed with special anti-sacramental significance as a tool or food of Satan. A sacrament is an outward and visible sign of an inward and spiritual grace; this was an outward and visible sign of an inward and spiritual rebellion. It became the focal point of a possible joining with the rebellion, an opportunity to assert, "Not God's will, but *mine* be done!" This became the motto of the rebellion, and sin entered the human race.

Adam Represents the Human Race

When Adam took the fruit of rebellion, he was not just acting on his own. He was the representative man, acting on behalf of the whole human race. When Adam eats, we are all brought into this rebellion. Adam had a real choice to obey, but now we are all swept into the rebellion and are born with sinful natures, a tendency toward sin, and a physical and spiritual inertia driving us toward death. Every day, we confirm by our choices that this is, indeed, our natural state. We are constantly battling this proclivity to sin and self-will. As Paul put it, we are now all dead in our transgressions (see Ephesians 2:1–5). Fear, lies, deception, self-centeredness, shame, and death have entered our human experience, and in just the next chapter of Genesis, we already witness the first murder.

The first sin was like a virus on a computer system, which spreads to the entire network. It has to be professionally removed because the computer cannot remove it on its own; it can't heal itself. This virus has affected all of us, and we cannot work back to where we were or restore ourselves to our previous state through good works.

Someone once said that the most vital life lessons are learned by the time we get through kindergarten. Think about that famous little nursery rhyme which we all know:

Humpty Dumpty sat on the wall;
Humpty Dumpty had a great fall.
All the king's horses and all the king's men
Couldn't put Humpty together again.

That little poem summarizes the basic message of Genesis 3:1–7. We have fallen from holiness, and we have partaken of the anti-sacrament. There is nothing we can do to put this right on our own. We are hopelessly broken, and no one on earth—not all the king's horses or all the king's men, not all the forces of humanity—can put us together again.

The gospel that God unveils is about a plan that He initiates to provide a way, not only to put us back together again, but to make us sons and daughters of God. Unless we fully grasp the gravity of sin and the seriousness of our condition before God, we will never hear the good news of what God has done to save us. Do you realize this day what a great gulf exists between God's holiness and our sinfulness?

Jesus, Lord of all creation, stepping into time and space;
Giving in Your incarnation hope to all the human race.

CHAPTER 2

Christ, the Second Adam

Romans 5:1–21

The opening chapters of Genesis teach us that we are hopelessly broken, and no human power can put us back together
again. In Adam, we have all rebelled, partaken of the anti-
sacrament, severed our relationship with God, and yelled in
his face, "Not Your will, but *mine* be done!" Paul reminded us
of this connection with Adam when he said, "Sin entered the
world through one man, and death through sin, and in this
way death came to all men, because all sinned" (5:12). Adam,
unlike us, did not have a tendency toward sin, and through a
real choice, he chose to become a sinner. In that act, he was a
representative man whose actions had consequences for the
entire race. We, on the other hand, do not have the capacity

to live a life apart from sin. We are born sinners, and we sin as a natural outgrowth of our sin nature.

How Adam's Sin Affects All

The central question, then, is: How did Adam's sin make us sinners? What is the relationship between Adam's sin and our condemnation? You may think it's not fair that Adam's choices, thousands of years ago, are affecting you now. You may wish to be your own Adam or Eve, to be free of the connection we share with those first human beings. After all, it's just not fair. Be careful, though, because Paul is laying the groundwork for a very important doctrine in the Bible: that of *vicarious* action, something done on your behalf apart from your initiative. If you cannot be connected to Adam and his choices thousands of years ago, then you can also have no part in the actions of Jesus Christ, who also lived thousands of years ago and did things on your behalf, just as Adam did. The knife cuts both ways.

Verse 12 says that sin entered the world and death through sin because all sinned. Through Adam, sin entered the world, and death (both physical and spiritual) is the greatest emblem of sin. When Paul said "because all sinned," however, he was not saying that death comes to all because we have all subsequently sinned as the generations have unfolded. It is true that we have all sinned and confirmed Adam's choice to be part of the rebellion, but what Paul meant is that we all sinned in Adam. In other words, you were there in the garden and sinned with Adam. This is a hard doctrine for modern people, especially Americans, who do not have a very strong sense of how we are connected to one another or to past generations. The Bible, on the other hand, presents the concept that you are not just an individual; inside of your loins reside all the future generations, or progeny, who will come forth from you. When Adam sinned, the Bible teaches that you were present in the body, or the loins, of Adam. In that way, we actually participated in the sin of Adam.

YOU ARE HERE

If you've ever gone shopping in a large mall and referred to the maps that show the whole scheme of the mall, you must have noticed that in one spot on the map is a small, helpful sign that reads, "You are here." Without it, you could not orient yourself in relation to the full map. When you read this account of Adam and Eve, you should notice that the Bible puts a little sign there, reading, "You are here." When Adam and Eve take the fruit and eat of the anti-sacrament, you are here. When they shout at God, "Not Your will, but *mine* be done," you are here. In one fell swoop, Satan got the whole human race to disobey God.

What's more, we have all confirmed Adam's sin in our own lives, choosing our own will every day over the will of

17

God. As Augustine said, "We are sinners by birth and by choice." How can the human race be rescued out of the rebellion and avoid inevitable condemnation when, without exception, everyone is bound to become a part of it? The only way is to bring another Adam into the world, someone who will once again have the choice to obey or disobey, but this time will get it right. We have to find a way to go back and rewrite that first chapter of the human story. But how is that possible? God knows that the whole human race is ineligible, so it couldn't be an inside job. What if He did an outside job, a rebooting of the whole system, a radical entrance of God Himself into the story of human history? He had to find a way to enter the human race in an abnormal way that would not pass on the sin nature, and yet would still be fully human. So Christ was born of a virgin into the human race as the second Adam.

How Christ's Atonement Affects All

Satan tried desperately to tempt Jesus, but at every point of assault, Jesus, unlike Adam, chose to obey God, to reject the forces of the rebellion, to live without sin. He had the capacity as the God-Man to sin or not to sin; He could have chosen to disobey the Father, but He didn't. If we trust in Christ, then by the same vicariousness by which we were implicated in Adam's sin, we are now implicated in Christ's obedience. We are now part of a new race of redeemed humanity, headed by Christ, rather than the old race condemned under Adam. As Romans 5:19 says, "For just as through the disobedience of the one man the many were made sinners, so also through the obedience of the one man the many will be made righteous." The first Adam committed one sin and brought judgment on the whole human race. The second Adam bore millions of acts of rebellion in His body on the cross, but was able to offer a way out by providing a perfect atoning sacrifice. Before, when we read the story of Adam and his rebellion against God, we saw the sign reading, "You are here." Now, as followers of Christ, when we read the account of the fall, that little sign isn't there. Instead, as we flip through the pages of the New Testament, we find that sign again and again throughout the life of Jesus. When Jesus is tempted in the desert and declares that He will love the Lord God and serve Him only, *you are here*. When Christ confronts the demonic world, exercising authority over the rebellion, *you are here*. You are in Christ as He obeyed, just as you were once in Adam as he disobeyed! In every situation where the first Adam disobeyed, the second Adam obeyed. Whenever the first Adam said no to God, this Adam said yes. In Christ, the entire history of the human race is being rewritten, and now we *can* turn the clock back and get it right.

The final test culminates in the garden of Gethsemane. The whole thing started in the garden of Eden, and now here we are in another garden, facing the same question of obedience. After a lifetime of choosing the Father's will above His own, is Jesus prepared to choose God's will in this final test? Is He ready to take upon Himself the sins of the whole world, to suffer separation from His Father, to bear the wrath of God for all the sins of humanity from Adam until the end of time? This is the most intense moment of human history; the decision of Jesus at this very moment, on His knees, sweating blood, and crying out to God, holds the whole fate of the human race in the balance. Finally, Jesus says the words that have changed the world: "Not *My* will, but Yours be done." In that moment, Jesus reverses the motto of the rebellion and turns the tables on all the powers of evil. And yes, there is a little sign there that reads, *"You are here!"* Man's great "no" of rebellion is being swallowed up in Christ's great "yes" of obedience.

As we continue to watch the unfolding story, we see Jesus Christ suffer the full judgment of God and cry out, as the sky grows dark and the earth splits open, "My God, My God, why have You forsaken Me?" We want to scream out, "It's not fair!" It's not fair for this innocent man who never sinned to suffer like this. It's not fair for the Son of God to experience the judgment that we deserved. No, it's not fair—praise God! This is grace. This is the Christian gospel. No one has ever loved like this or made choices like this before, and yet through our veil of tears, we see at the cross the little sign reading, "You are here." By God's grace, we can be in Christ just as we used to be in Adam. Everyone must decide whose headship they are under: that of the rebellion in Adam, or that of obedience in Christ. A new way has been purchased by the blood of God's only Son, a way to escape the curse of the first Adam. Praise be to God for His indescribable gift!

> *Adam, as we share your nature, like you we stand bound in sin;*
> *Jesus, now our second Adam—new creation you begin!*

CHAPTER 3

God's Global Plan to Abraham

Genesis 12:1–9

You may be wondering why there was such a huge time gap between the first and second Adam. If, after all, the first Adam condemned the whole human race to die, and if there was no way out of it until God sent a second Adam into the world, why didn't God do it a week after Adam fell rather than wait thousands of years before sending Christ into the world? The first reason is that the consequences of that original sin were so great that it would take a very long time to prepare the human race properly for the entrance of the second Adam. In order for the human race to grasp what God was going to do, there were many crucial elements that had to be in place: the holiness of God, the sinfulness of man, the concept of sacrifice, the priesthood, and many others. The coming of Christ is like a great spiritual banquet; everything must be prepared in advance, and that takes time.

The second reason for the huge time gap is that God is the Lord of time, and therefore is not bound by it. Abraham and the other Old Testament saints were saved in the same way that you and I are saved. We look back several thousands of years to the incarnation, death, and resurrection of Christ, and God miraculously moves us back through time so we are now spiritually in Christ, just as we had been in Adam. But God can do this miracle in both directions! Abraham looked forward to God's provision and trusted God to move him miraculously forward in time so that he also was in Christ through faith. For the Lord, there is no major difference between our looking back and Abraham looking forward because everyone is looking toward Christ, and both are trusting in God's provision.

God's Redemption Plan

So even though it would take a long time, God had already put His plan of salvation into place and promised that someday the second Adam would come to crush the serpent's head (see Genesis 3:15). In the meantime, He would continue to raise up faithful ones who would look forward, trusting in God's provision. After the fall, there was a blitz of generations before we come to the story of Noah, a faithful one in the time of much unfaithfulness. The biblical narrative then blitzes forward through many more descendants, who are learning, just as little children do, that God is far beyond what their towers can reach or their minds can grasp; that they are sinful, that God will judge, but that He will also provide. These first eleven chapters of Genesis show the human race in its infancy, learning basic lessons about God. Finally, we arrive at chapter 12, and the narrative slows down. It goes from near warp speed to a slow plod. Now, we are entering the timeline of human history and focusing on the life of one person rather than a historical timeline. God is about to begin with one man, and it is through this man that God is going to raise up the people who will bring Christ into the world.

GOD'S PROMISE TO ABRAHAM

The covenant with Abraham in chapter 12 reminds us that God has not forgotten His original plan. His plan is to establish a human family who will live in loving relationship and communion with Him. This is what God intended for the whole human race when He told Adam and Eve to be fruitful, multiply, and fill the earth. Often, we make the mistake of thinking God's main plan is to redeem people because that dominates so much of the Bible. But His plan of redemption is necessary only in order to get us back to the original goal, which is fellowship, communion, worship, and ruling and reigning with Christ.

According to tradition, Abraham's father was not only an idol worshipper, but also an idol maker. So God takes the initiative. While we were still sinners, Christ died for us; while Abraham was still in the bosom of the rebellion, God took the initiative and called him forth. God called him to step out in faith and receive His provision, to leave the cycle of sin, death, and judgment, and listen to God's plan. This cycle of sin had reached its peak in the Tower of Babel, right before the call of Abraham. The world system that it embodied touted the paradigm of settling down (11:2), building a city or monument for ourselves, and making our own names great (11:4). God's call turned these worldly goals on their heads, asking Abraham to live out a new paradigm, one diametrically opposed to that of the old order. He called Abraham to uproot, to be a pilgrim; not to build a city for himself, but instead to build a people and to wait for a city whose maker and builder would be God (see Hebrews 11:8–10); and to trust his name and his progeny to the Lord, for the Lord would be the one who would make his name great.

> "I will make you into a great nation, and I will bless you; I will make your name great, and you will be a blessing. I will bless those who bless you, and whoever curses you I will curse; and all peoples on earth will be blessed through you." (Gen. 12:2–3)

Since this covenant is restated over and over again, we see that there are three main parts to it: personal, numerical blessing to Abraham; national, geographic blessing to the nation of Israel; and spiritual blessing to all nations. As we continue through the pages of Genesis, we see the personal and national blessings blossoming through Abraham's descendants. In Genesis 22, 26, and 38, we read the restatement of these promises to Abraham, Isaac, and Jacob. But the bottom line of the promise, and of God's ultimate plan, is to bless *all* nations through the line of Abraham. *Nations* does not mean countries, but people groups; not politics, but peoples; not geography, but ethnicity. All people groups on earth will be blessed through this promise to Abraham. When we read the Old Testament, we are not reading some old, vague book about Israel that has little to do with us as believers today. No, this story has everything to do with us. When we read the Old Testament, we are vicariously reading our own history, because even if we are not ethnic Jews, we are part of God's plan from the beginning, His plan to redeem *all* the nations. The church is not some separate plan B once Israel rebelled against the covenant; the church was the original plan of all peoples united in Christ by a blessing that was too big for any one people.

The bottom line of the covenant, then, is about restoration, not just forgiveness of sins. It's about ruling and reigning with Christ, raising up families from every nation, people, and language to worship and love the Lord Jesus Christ, to whom belongs all glory and honor and praise. At the end of the Bible, the apostle John had a vision that was recorded in dramatic detail: "After this I looked, and there before me was a great multitude that no one could count, from every nation, tribe, people and language, standing before the throne and in front of the Lamb" (Rev. 7:9). This passage should remind us that God keeps His promises. He promised that in the seed of Abraham He would bless all nations, and now, in the final vision of John, we see all the nations of the world standing before the throne of God and under His blessing!

We should be encouraged to remember that God is on the throne! He is bringing all of His purposes about in His time and in His way. We do not need to feel afraid or to succumb to those inner voices that tell us that things are out of control. Instead, we place our trust anew in God's grace and power. Know that God keeps His promises! He is unfolding a glorious plan that involves you and me, and all who have trusted Him, ruling and reigning with Christ in heavenly realms. So we can lift our heads high this day and know that God has great plans for us and for His world. Christ will return, and He will create a new heaven and a new earth, and together we will reign with Him for eternity. Indeed, "no eye has seen, no ear has heard, no mind has conceived what God has prepared for those who love him" (1 Cor. 2:9)!

> *Abraham, a covenant was made with you by means of faith;*
> *Jesus brings that faith's fulfillment, grafted in from every race.*

CHAPTER 4

Abraham Meets the King-Priest Melchizedek

Genesis 14:17–20; Psalm 110:4; Hebrews 7:1–17

We are now beginning to see the shape of God's plan of redemption unfolding in history as recorded in Scripture. A key feature of Christ's fulfillment of the Old Testament is that He would come and be the final high priest. This emerges in the book of Genesis in a rather unexpected way. Genesis 14 opens with the account of a regional conflict that pits five local kings against four other kings who oversee small areas of the region. The four kings defeated the five kings, who fled with all their men, allowing Kedorlaomer and his allies to capture everything—cattle, sheep, women, and children—anything and everything. In the ancient world these were considered the spoils of war since no soldier was paid for his service. You may recall that Abraham's (Abram at this point in the story) nephew Lot had decided to live in Sodom (see Genesis 13), which was a notoriously wicked city. Sodom was one of the little kingdoms defeated in this conflict, so Kedorlaomer and his allies had captured Abraham's nephew Lot and taken all of his belongings. Abraham heard that his nephew had been taken captive, so he took 318 of his best-trained men and set out on a hundred-mile pursuit and finally overtook them way up in the north. Abraham knew he didn't have the forces to defeat them in a pitched battle, so he divided his men to attack them at night and routed them. The fleeing kings abandoned their spoils, and Abraham recaptured everything that had been taken. He returned home with his nephew Lot and his possessions, and all the captured slaves and livestock.

Melchizedek Enters the Scene

In Genesis 14:18 a very odd thing happens. It is so odd that the Jewish people ruminated over this for centuries. A man named Melchizedek, who was not a part of this conflict, comes to Abraham. There are six things about this encounter that were considered quite strange.

(1) His name is Melchizedek, which means "king of righteousness," or perhaps "one who worships or honors the king of the righteousness." Who is this king of righteousness?

(2) He is the king of Salem, which means "peace" and is an early reference to what would later be called Jerusalem.

(3) He is both a king and a priest. In verse 18 he is called king of Salem and "priest of God Most High." Israel would have kings and priests, but never in one person. The kings came from the line of Judah, but the priests from the line of Levi. This is very strange, indeed.

(4) He emerges with no calling card or proper introduction. He just comes out of the blue. Everybody knows, even the people that have never actually read the Bible, that the Scriptures are full of genealogies, which tell how a certain person begat a person who begat another person, and so forth. Family lineages (who you are, who is your daddy, and where do you come from) were very important things in the ancient world. It was like your calling card. No one said, "Hello. My name is so-and-so." Rather, they said, "Hello. My name is so-and-so, the son of so-and-so, the grandson of so-and-so, who was victorious in this or that battle, or who performed some great feat." Everyone was connected. There was no personal identity or personal autonomy as it is known in the modern world. It is because of the absence of information about Melchizedek that the Jewish people speculated quite a bit about who he might have been. We don't know who his father or mother was, nothing of his genealogy, either his ancestors or progeny, and we don't even know how old he was.

(5) He brings out bread and wine and blesses Abraham, not the other way around. Bread and wine are the primordial elements of life that would someday reemerge at the Passover and at the Eucharist. Melchizedek offered these gifts and this blessing by invoking the name of God Himself, *El Elyon*, a title that is used twenty-eight times in the Old Testament:

> Blessed be Abram by [*El Elyon*] God Most High, Creator of heaven and earth. And praise be to [*El Elyon*] God Most High, who delivered your enemies into your hand. (vv. 19–20)

(6) Abraham tithed 10 percent of all the spoils of war to Melchizedek. Genesis 14:20 records that "Abram gave him a tenth of everything." It was customary to tithe 10 percent of the spoils to a king. The great patriarch Abraham, the fountainhead of monotheism and one of the most influential people in the history of the world, was tithing to this unknown priest-king named Melchizedek.

Biblical References Regarding a King-Priest

Psalm 110

The memory of this encounter stays with the Jewish people for a thousand years—all the way to the time of David. David, as you know, wrote many of the Psalms, several of which are known as coronation psalms (i.e., psalms to celebrate the coronation of a king). In Psalm 110, David seems to prophetically prefigure not merely his own son's coronation, but also great David's greater Son, the true messianic king who was to come and redeem Israel. Psalm 110 is a coronation psalm for a king, and yet it extols the figure as a "priest forever, in the order of Melchizedek" (v. 4). For a people who only knew of the order of Aaron and the Levitical priesthood, this meant that the prefigured Messiah would be both king and priest. David is aware that this is a major dilemma that must be resolved. How can the Messiah be both high king *and* high priest? Judah is the kingly line; Levi is the priestly line. The two lineages are separate, so how can the Messiah fulfill both? But David remembers the story of Melchizedek from millennia earlier. In Psalm 110, David hints at the solution by stating that there was a priesthood that was earlier than the tribe of Levi which dates back to Abraham, who is the great-grandfather of all the tribes. It is in Psalm 110 that we learn of the order of Melchizedek.

Zechariah 6

This hope appears again in Zechariah 6:9–15. There the Lord instructs Zechariah to take the high priest, whose name, amazingly, is the Hebrew name for Jesus—Joshua—and to declare that his name is the Branch and that he will rebuild the temple, the dwelling place of God, and will be clothed with majesty and sit on a throne. He will be a priest on the throne, bringing harmony between the two: the kingship and the priesthood. Again, in Israel, no one could ever be both a king and a priest. Abraham's grandson Jacob had twelve sons who became the twelve tribes of Jacob—two of his sons were Judah and Levi. It was from Judah that the kings would come, and it was from Levi that God would raise up the priests. The sons of Levi and the sons of Judah were prohibited from intertribal marriage, so no one—even the Messiah it seemed, could become both a priest and a king.

HEBREWS 7

Another thousand years go by and the writer of the book of Hebrews explains the whole thing with clarity. He is seeking to explain how Jesus can serve as the great high priest of the Christian faith even though He is from the tribe of Judah: "For it is clear that our Lord descended from Judah, and in regard to that tribe Moses said nothing about priests" (Heb. 7:14).

The book of Hebrews goes to great lengths to explain that there was an earlier priestly order that precedes and trumps the tribe of Levi—the order of Melchizedek! He then tells us all the ways this priesthood is superior to the Levitical priesthood. There are three main reasons.

The Superiority of Melchizedek's Priesthood

First, it is a *permanent priesthood*. The text says, "You are a priest *forever* in the order of Melchizedek" (Heb. 7:17, emphasis mine). The Levitical priests always died and their priesthood expired and was passed on to someone else. But this priest, this messiah, was declared to be a priest forever, in the order of Melchizedek! This permanence is even sealed with a divine oath: "The Lord has sworn and will not change his mind: 'You are a priest forever.'"

Second, Abraham *tithed* to him, not the other way around. According to Jewish law, everyone tithed to support the Levitical priesthood because the Levites were not given their own territory. But Abraham tithed to Melchizedek and since all of Abraham's descendants are in his loins—in his body—then vicariously the entire tribe of Levi (Abraham's great-grandson) was there, tithing *in Abraham*. The lesser always tithes to the greater, and so the whole Levitical priesthood, through Abraham, was tithing to the superior priesthood of Melchizedek.

Third, the priesthood of Melchizedek is greater than the Levitical priesthood because of the *character* of the two parties involved. The Levites were themselves sinners. They had to sacrifice for themselves before they could sacrifice for the sins of the people, just as ordained ministers receive communion before they give it today. This is not merely symbolic solidarity, but the declaration that ministers and priests are also sinners. But Jesus was a priest without sin, and not because of some human ancestry or lineage, but because of the righteous indestructibility of his life!

Melchizedek is a type of Christ who demonstrates how Jesus Christ is both King and Priest. We have already celebrated how Christ is the second Adam, and here we see Christ as the Great High Priest. All the priests of the Old Testament were prefiguring this Great High Priest.

My brothers and sisters, in Jesus Christ we have the complete fulfillment of the whole Jewish priesthood. Indeed, the whole priesthood prefigured the one true High Priest who was to come, Jesus Christ. In the old order, people had to confess their sins to a priest. But with Christ as our High Priest, we can boldly and directly enter into the glorious presence of God (Hebrews 10:19–22). Jesus is the intermediary who stands in the gap and intercedes for us, representing us before God as our Great High Priest!

Three Signs that the Church Doesn't Understand Christ's Priesthood

I fear that in our day we have misunderstood the doctrines of the priesthood of Christ, and the priesthood of all believers. There can only be a priesthood of all believers if we are abiding in Christ, who is the Great High Priest. There are three signs in the contemporary church that demonstrate that we do not comprehend this doctrine.

SIGN 1: CAVALIER CASUALNESS

We have turned the priesthood of all believers into a God-is-my-pal theme, where we somehow can lightly and casually saunter into the presence of God with a cup of coffee and a donut in our hand. Pastors, in their desire to be user-friendly, may inadvertently be teaching their congregations that coming into God's presence is no big deal. But coming before the living God is always a big deal. Prayers of confession and repentance have almost disappeared from the contemporary church. This is a sign of a sick church, not a spiritual one. We should never confuse confidence in Christ with casualness before the living God.

SIGN 2: PRESUMPTUOUS ENTITLEMENT

We are all aware of how an entitlement mentality has crept into our society. Tragically, the church has not been exempt from this. When God doesn't do things according to our feeble sense of justice and morality, we may find ourselves saying, "He had better explain Himself to our satisfaction, or we will go our own way." The church's explanation for suffering in the world has always been rooted in the power of the only true innocent sufferer hanging on a cross. Our trust in God is rooted in the High Priesthood of Christ, who is both the promise and the keeper of the promise, both priest

37

and sacrifice. Today, we seem to have lost our voice because we have come to see ourselves as innocent sufferers. We have largely agreed with the unbelieving world that God is cruel and unjust and silent in the face of suffering. We must recapture the great truth that Jesus Christ is the only true holy priest and innocent sufferer. God doesn't explain suffering; He takes it upon Himself on the cross.

SIGN 3: RELIGIOUS FUNCTIONARIES

The contemporary church has turned the pastorate into a class of religious functionaries. Many pastors in the church have become like Old Testament priests who perform all the proper rituals and are asked to show up at funerals and weddings to carry out religious duties. A new human priesthood has become superimposed over the priesthood of all believers. I do not mean to diminish the importance of the leadership role that is uniquely filled by those set apart for pastoral ministry. My point is that their role is not to perform religious functions, but to equip the whole church to do the work of ministry. Jesus alone is the Great High Priest, and it is in Him that all Christians are his priests and ministers.

My prayer is that we all would capture a renewed glimpse into the holy mystery of Jesus Christ, the great Paschal Priest who alone has passed through the heavens and through great cost brought us into the ineffable presence of the living

God. Once we are in Christ, then there is a wonderful joy and even boldness that can accompany our confident procession into His kingly presence. He wants us to delight in Him. He has called us sons and daughters. But all of these treasures are only possible if we keep at the center of our faith, Jesus Christ, who alone is God's Great High Priest.

> *Levi paid through Abraham a tithe unto the kingly priest;*
> *Jesus, Most High Priest forever, interceding without cease.*

CHAPTER 5

Jehovah Jireh—God Will Provide

Genesis 22:1–18

Fact, Faith, and Feeling

One of the most familiar images used in evangelism when I was in high school was this image developed by Campus Crusade for Christ (today CRU). It was trying to establish the point that the historical *fact* of what God has done redemptively is like the engine of salvation. It is what pulls the whole thing. The synergy with us comes when we place our *faith* in what God has done, thus the second coal car. This was often connected to the famous sinner's prayer. Finally, the chart was meant to show that our *feelings* (meaning our emotions) may or may not be present, and you shouldn't rely upon them—they are like the caboose. They are often present, but they should not be confused with the engine.

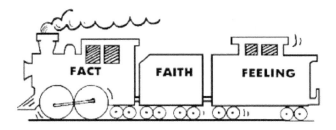

Long before Campus Crusade, these three terms were prominent in nineteenth-century evangelistic preaching, and perhaps they are perennial tensions in the gospel. I have seen this picture for forty years, and I must confess that it took me about thirty-five of those years before I actually noticed and reflected on the most neglected part of this image. In fact, as I recall, it was never even mentioned in Crusade tracts where this diagram appeared, nor can I find references to it in nineteenth-century evangelistic preaching. It is the tracks! Trains cannot run without tracks.

It was on May 10, 1869, that the great Central Pacific Railroad and the Union Railroad finally met, connecting the eastern rail with the western rail and creating the first transcontinental rail passage in America. A decade was spent laying 1,776 miles of track so the railroad could run from east to west. Tracks are essential for trains. If I can press the image, God's great train of redemption cannot run without tracks. This is the reason why Jesus was not sent into the world in Genesis 3. After all, if the only hope of redemption is the coming of Christ, then why not send Him in Genesis 3? Instead, we get a vague prophecy, a little seed of hope in Genesis 3:15: "he will crush your head, and you will strike his heel." It turns out that this entire devotional book is really about God laying the tracks so the train of redemption can come into the world. Without the big railroad ties of law, sacrifice, priesthood, vicariousness, faith, covenant, and so forth, the gospel train cannot run.

Laying the Tracks for Faith and Redemption

Tracks are laid in multiple ways in the Bible. In the big picture, God works to establish certain truths about humanity and Himself, which are essential for our receiving the message. But He also calls us to lay tracks in our own individual lives. These tracks prepare us for God's redemptive work in our own lives. Many of you have been asked to walk through some very painful experiences. You have had to face suffering, difficulty, and even the silence of God. You have languished before God, trying to understand the facts of it, or the place of your faith in it, not to mention the endless vacillations of feelings, and you may have missed the deeper point that God was laying tracks in your life. You were being prepared to receive something that you otherwise could not receive.

Genesis 22 is the ultimate story of tracks being laid, both in the big picture as Abraham enters into God's unfolding plan of redemption, and also in the life of Abraham himself. In Genesis 22, God asks Abraham to do the most difficult thing anyone could ever be asked: "Take your son, your only son, whom you love—Isaac—and go to the region of Moriah. Sacrifice him there as a burnt offering on a mountain I will show you" (v. 2). This is a doubly shocking text. The sheer notion of child sacrifice is an absolute abominable act of evil (which the Law later made explicit). But the second shock is that it seems like such a dramatic reversal of what has been unfolding up to this point in the Genesis narrative. Abraham was promised an heir and great descendants. Finally, in Genesis 21 Isaac was born, when Abraham was one hundred years old. There is no time for a rerun; the redemptive clock is running, and the child of promise has finally come. Isaac is the physical embodiment of and fulfillment of all the divine promises; hope is now kindled, faith is more confident, trust is on the rise! Then, out of the blue, God says to take Isaac and sacrifice him. The whole thing is jarring, to say the least. But this is the climax in a series of faith tests. This is not about pitting Abraham's love for God against his love for Isaac. This is a test of Abraham's faith and trust in God precisely because he loves Isaac. In fact, it is Abraham's love of Isaac upon which the whole text is predicated. But for Abraham to be called the father of faith, he must be tested and found true at the highest level. Genesis 22 would not be possible without the tracks being laid from Genesis 12 onward.

TEST 1: LESSON OF THE BONDS OF FAMILY AND PLACE

In Genesis 12, we read about God's original covenant with Abraham. We need to stop and think about what a powerful test this covenant was for Abraham and his family: "Go from your country, your people and your father's household to the land I will show you" (v. 1). This is the test of geography and the familial bonds of family. The original covenant of Genesis 12 is built on the foundation of a test. Leaving your home and your parents and stepping out into the unknown is very difficult. Two of the biggest pulls in our life are geography and family. It is not easy to leave either. Jesus reminds us of this in Matthew 10:37. It is faith that brought Abraham from Ur of the Chaldees to Haran to Canaan. And it is faith that brought you to where you are today. Abraham obeyed, and thus the first tracks were laid so the train of faith could advance.

TEST 2: LESSON OF PROVISIONS

The second test is the test of provisions and is found in Genesis 14. After Abraham defeats the four kings, he ends up with considerable spoils of war. In fact, it was enough to make him a very wealthy man. But God had promised to make him a great man. Abraham refused to take even a "thread or the strap of a sandal" (v. 23). Otherwise, he told the king of Sodom, someday you will say that you made Abraham rich. Abraham is learning to trust God for his provision. He passes the test, another section of track is laid, and the train of faith moves even deeper into Abraham's life. Many of you have had to trust God for your provision. It is one of the biggest tests of faith, which is why Jesus highlights it again in the Sermon on the Mount.

TEST 3: LESSON OF COLLABORATION

The first two tests were successful, but the third test is a failure in the life of Abraham (at least the first time around). But this is also a great reminder that even when we fail, God still teaches us through our mistakes as well as our successes.

The third test is the test of collaboration. God's plan of redemption involves our participation. God always makes the first move, but we are called to respond and join Him in His plan. The nature of this cooperation has been a long-standing debate in the life of the church. There are those who shrink at the very idea that we have any role to play whatsoever in our salvation or, for that matter, the redemption of the world. As one well-known author put it, the only thing we bring to the plan of redemption is our sin. This approach collapses all of salvation down to our justification, and renders us passive observers of God's work and passive recipients of an alien righteousness. This tends to make our justification the whole story of salvation, rather than just the first half of the story of our salvation. But the other error is the impulse that tends to believe God's promises and then try to make it happen through our own strength. This error is perhaps best summed up in the well-intentioned but erroneous bumper sticker: *God is my copilot*. God is many things, but He is not our copilot. It can be hard for us to remember that we have no ministry apart from our participation in His ministry in the world. He is the central actor in the grand drama of redemption. We are *His* co-laborers; *His* helpers in the vineyard.

Abraham was taken outside by God on a beautiful starry night and told to look up at the stars and see if he could count them. That would be the number of his descendants! This is a powerful moment. This is the passage (Gen. 15) where we are told that "Abram believed the LORD, and he credited it to him as righteousness" (v. 6). But then in the very next chapter, we see that Abraham saw his barren wife, her advancing years, and he decided to help God out. God became his copilot. He decided to use Sarah's maidservant, Hagar, to achieve his promised descendants. This is what brought Ishmael into the world. God appears to Abraham again in Genesis 17 and reminds him that He will accomplish this covenant as He promised, through Sarah. This is when Abram is renamed Abraham, Sarai is renamed Sarah, and Abraham is reminded that the covenant will come through their descendants. The son's name will be Isaac.

It is in Genesis 18 that Abraham finally learns the lesson. He is given a strange test. God has decided to bring judgment against Sodom and Gomorrah. It is God's judgment, but He asks Abraham what his part is going to be in this. Will he be a passive observer, or will he enter into the anguish of the judgment with God? Abraham enters into a kind of Eastern marketplace-type bargaining and haggling with God. "Lord, what if there are fifty righteous, will you destroy the city?" God agrees to spare the city for the sake of fifty righteous. Abraham goes on to bargain for forty-five, forty, thirty, twenty, and finally ten. Abraham is learning that the redemption of the world is done collaboratively or synergistically with us as the redeemed. It is God's work—His act of judgment, and His act of redemption, that He alone unfolds in the world, but He has chosen to include Abraham in that work.

FINAL TEST 4: TEST OF ABSOLUTE TRUST

Genesis 22 is the test of absolute trust. It is this test that will accredit Abraham as the father of faith. It is only because the tracks have been laid in the previous three tests that this final test is possible. The text says, quite openly, that

God decided to test Abraham. The reader, at least, knows from the outset that this is a test of faith. Throughout the passage we meet one who trusts God. He knows the promise is that through Isaac the blessing will come. This command seems to contradict that, but Abraham has learned to trust. Hebrews 11:17–19 gives us an inspired insight into the inner reasoning of Abraham: "By faith Abraham, when God tested him, offered Isaac as a sacrifice. He who had embraced the promises was about to sacrifice his one and only son, even though God had said to him, 'It is through Isaac that your offspring will be reckoned.' Abraham reasoned that God could even raise the dead, and so in a manner of speaking he did receive Isaac back from death."

Abraham placed the wood on Isaac's back and they made their way to Mount Moriah, the very spot that would someday be the site of the temple and the Holy of Holies. Notice how silent and obedient Isaac is through the whole event. The only words are those of faith when Isaac says to his father, "Father, I see the wood and the fire. But, where is the lamb?" Abraham simply responds with "Jehovah Jireh"— God will provide. Isaac is bound. He is placed on the wood. Abraham raises the knife, and then come those beautiful words: *Abraham, Abraham. Do not lay a hand on the boy. Now I know that you fear God.*

It is because of this act of obedience that Abraham is known as the father of faith.

The Faithfulness of God

Genesis 22 is the culmination of God's work in the life of Abraham, but there is another narrative unfolding. The chapter is not just about the faith of Abraham; it also about the faithfulness of God. We have seen that God Himself is laying tracks for us all. Big tracks are being laid so that Christ can someday come into the world in the fullness of time. Without the great timbers of faith, of law, of priesthood, of substitutionary sacrifice, of judgment, of covenant, and so forth, the incarnation of Jesus Christ and His death on the cross would not have made sense. Genesis 22, from the perspective of the grand story of redemption, is like a great dress rehearsal for the actual drama of redemption. We should never forget that Abraham was not asked to do anything that God did not ask of Himself, because this story foreshadows the great passion of our Lord Jesus. God the Father sent His Son into the world. He allowed us to place wood on His back, a piece of wood known as a cross, and make His way to the place of sacrifice, where God offered up His Son, His only Son, whom He loved, for the sins of the world. It was the only way to break the power of darkness and to offer a way out of this self-destructive rebellion in which we are all trapped. This is why when Jesus came into the world, the gospel of John, verse 29, records John the Baptist saying those powerful words, "Look, the Lamb of God who takes away the sin of the world!" This great drama is about more than the faith of Abraham; it is about the faithfulness of God. It is about more than Abraham's love of God; it is about God's tremendous love for you and me. Abraham's sacrifice is the great foreshadowing of God's great sacrifice in Jesus Christ. Substitutionary atonement is first seen here, later enshrined in the sacrificial system, but finally, in the mystery of faith and in the fullness of time, fulfilled in Jesus Christ. Abraham is known redemptively as the father of faith, but even that exalted title is only pointing to the real central figure of redemption—Jesus Christ—who stands as the author and perfecter of all faith, including the faith of Abraham.

> *In the sacrifice of Isaac, faith was proved and grace was found;*
> *Jesus is God's sacrifice where grace and justice both abound.*

CHAPTER 6

Moses: The Great Deliverer

Exodus 14:26–31; Hosea 11:1; Matthew 2:13–15;
1 Corinthians 5:7–8; 10:1–4; Hebrews 3:1–6

We are continuing to unfold some of the great contours of redemptive history as Christ, in the fullness of time, becomes the second Adam, Keeper of the Covenant, Sacrifice, Prophet, Priest, King, New Lawgiver, New Israel, and Suffering Servant. We still have a way to go in this journey, but we are beginning to see the amazing way in which Jesus is pre-figured by the Old Testament.

God Uses an Unlikely Leader

In this chapter we move to the third of our Old Testament figures, Moses, an unlikely leader who becomes the great deliverer and lawgiver of Israel, a prophet unlike any other, whom the Lord knew face to face (see Deuteronomy 34:10). Moses was born at a dangerous time, and saved from Pharaoh's decree that all baby boys born to the Hebrews be thrown into the Nile. He was placed into a basket and rescued by Pharaoh's daughter and raised in the very courts of Pharaoh. He was given the best education and training, but he never forgot the suffering of his people in slavery to the Egyptians. One day, he saw an Egyptian beating a Hebrew slave, one of his own people. Moses glanced to the left and to the right, and then he killed the Egyptian and hid him in the sand (see Exodus 2:11-12).

Even though Moses was being prepared to be a deliverer, he thought he could exercise that longing in his own way. By killing the Egyptian, he tried to make it happen through his own strength, resources, and ingenuity. God took him to school: the desert. In the last chapter we traced how God laid tracks for Abraham, to prepare him for his role as the father of faith, culminating in Genesis 22. For forty years, Moses lived in the wilderness of Midian while God humbled him and prepared him to be His true deliverer. It is only after forty years that he is ready, and God finally appears to him in the burning bush and formally calls him to deliver Israel. God is the one who took the initiative this time. He reminded Moses that He had also seen the misery of His people and heard them crying out because of their slave drivers. He cares more than Moses ever could about their suffering, and He has come down to rescue them. Moses' three responses demonstrate that he has indeed changed during his years in the wilderness. God's school had truly taught him his own inadequacy to deliver the Israelites through his own power. First he asked, *Who am I that I should go?* God's response reminds him and us that this is God's unfolding plan. It is not about who Moses is, but who the Lord is. Moses' second question is, *What if they don't believe me?* God's answer is the staff in his hand, which miraculously turns into a snake. With this, God reminds Moses that the authority of the Lord goes with him. Third, Moses argued, *I am not eloquent of speech!* God answered that it is He who gave man his tongue, and that He will teach Moses what to say. He will give Moses His words. Equipped with the name of God, the authority of God, and the word of God, Moses is prepared to become Israel's leader in order to deliver them out of bondage, through the Red Sea, and eventually to Mount Sinai, where they are given the Ten Commandments, which represent the covenant between Yahweh and Israel.

God Continues to Lay the Tracks of Redemption through Moses

The Passover and Red Sea sequence become the great paradigm of deliverance for Israel. We will examine the Law in a later chapter and see how Christ is both the Law's fulfillment, and the new Lawgiver for the people of God. In this chapter we are going to focus on the great narrative of redemption: Passover to the Red Sea, and the birth of Israel as the people of God in covenant with Yahweh, not just a group of freed slaves.

The Passover and Exodus

The rescue from Egypt is a very long narrative from Exodus 7–12, culminating in the tenth and final plague, the death of the firstborn of all Egypt. Israel, too, would suffer this judgment unless they sacrificed the blood of a spotless lamb and placed that blood over the top and side of the door frame. If the blood was there, the death angel would pass over their home and they would be spared from judgment. Exodus 12:11 uses a very interesting phrase, "it is the Lord's Passover." He doesn't say, it is *your* Passover, but it is Yahweh's Passover. The term "Passover" at this point does not refer to a festival, although in this chapter the festival called Passover is instituted. The root idea behind Passover is focused on the victim of the night, which is the lamb. This is why it is the Lord's Passover—He is directing the entire basis for the deliverance in very detailed terms. The spotless lamb is the Lord's designated sacrificial victim. It is His night where He acts to deliver His people.

As Christians we recognize that this is yet another way that God laid the tracks to prepare us for the coming of

Christ into the world. When Paul said in 1 Corinthians 5:7 that "Christ, our Passover Lamb, has been sacrificed," he was making a theological connection between the spotless lamb and the blood on the door frames with the sacrifice of Jesus Christ and His blood, which delivers us from God's righteous judgment. Jesus Christ is the Passover Lamb. He is the designated victim who ultimately secures our redemption, both Jew and Gentile. Later, in 1 Corinthians 10, Paul compares the passing through the Red Sea to baptism. This was their baptism—their inauguration into the changed status from slaves to the people of God, just as baptism for us marks our transition from people enslaved to sin, to those who are partakers in all the privileges and promises of the people of God. The manna in the wilderness is Christ Himself (John 6:32–33). Paul even said that the rock from which the water flowed in the wilderness was Christ (see 1 Corinthians 10:4). You see, Christ's death and resurrection invades our present so that we too become caught up in His death and resurrection. We died with Christ; we were raised with Christ. This great central act of redemption moves backward through time as well, and in the mystery of the gospel, Christ is the Passover Lamb that was sacrificed. It was Christ's blood being placed on the door frames. It was He who led them through the Red Sea. He is the cloudy pillar by day and the fiery pillar by night. It is Christ alone who redeems the world. The early Jews who embraced Christ never had to leave the central act of Passover behind in order to embrace Christ. Rather, they saw that the new central historical act of redemption, the cross and resurrection, became part of the great plan of redemption. Rather than the Passover being left behind, it is instilled with new significance and it becomes part and parcel of the great act of redemption.

There are not multiple plans of redemption, but one great unfolding plan. Notice the redemptive movement that is taking place. In Genesis 12, God lays out from the start the ultimate vision, the reconciliation of all the families and nations of the earth. This is the whole foundation of the covenant with Abraham, which is repeated to Isaac and Jacob. God redeems the world by first electing Israel as the one redeemed nation, the firstfruits of His plan of global redemption through whom the messiah for all will come. But Israel is not faithful and forsakes the covenant. However, God is the great keeper of the covenant, so the movement goes from all nations, to Israel, to a remnant of Israel. But the remnant is also unable to keep the covenant, so, in God's plan Jesus Christ becomes the new Israel. Christ alone becomes the redeemer of the nations, even including the redemption of Egypt. The covenant says all nations, and that must include the peoples of Egypt, even though Egypt was the nation that held Israel in bondage and enslaved them. Throughout the Prophets, the idea of going back to Egypt was a sign of trusting in human strength, human resources. If you are an Egyptian, you can only imagine how difficult it is to find your place in the narrative of redemption.

JESUS REENACTS THE EXODUS

But remember in Matthew's gospel, immediately following the visit of the Magi, Matthew records the relocation of Joseph, Mary, and Jesus to Egypt (2:13–15). This is, of course, significant as Jesus reenacts the Exodus whereby the children of Israel came up out of Egypt. Matthew, in his gospel, even boldly declares that Jesus coming up out of Egypt was in fulfillment of Hosea 11:1, *"Out of Egypt I called my son."* Jesus is physically reenacting the Exodus in the same way that in the garden of Gethsemane he reenacted the original temptation in the garden of Eden. However, it should not be overlooked that in Matthew's gospel we find the transformation of Egypt from a symbol of oppression and bondage, to a nation that now protects and provides safe haven for the Messiah.[1] Now, Egypt is not oppressing God's people and thwarting God's plan, but becomes a critical player in God's plan by protecting the very life of the Messiah. Egypt's role as a haven for the Messiah is not only theologically powerful, but it helps to invigorate Israel's historical memory to the time long before their painful Egyptian bondage when Egypt provided a haven for Abraham (see Genesis 12:10). It is a refreshing testimony to the power of the gospel to reconcile all nations.

Jesus Becomes the New Israel and New Moses

The vision for all nations is reaffirmed, including Egypt. The movement from all nations to Israel, to a remnant of Israel, to finally just one man, Jesus Christ, who alone acts to redeem the world, is the basis for building the new people of God, the church of Jesus Christ, which then preaches the gospel to all nations, culminating in the fulfillment of the original promise to Abraham to bless all nations. This promise is finally realized in Revelation 7:9 when John sees men and women from every tribe, tongue, and people worshipping before the Lamb. So, the Passover-Exodus narrative prefigures the deliverance and sacrifice of Christ Himself and ultimately points to His gathering of all nations (not just Israel). He is the spotless Lamb, whose blood is shed for the redemption of the world. He comes out of Egypt, He lays His life down, and He is sacrificed as the final sacrifice, and through that one sacrifice, leads His peoples out of the bondage of sin and, in the process, redeems the world! Jesus is the Great Deliverer, the Passover Lamb sacrificed for our exodus out of the land of slavery. As Jesus said just before the famous John 3:16 passage, "Just as Moses lifted up the snake in the desert, so the Son of Man must be lifted up, that everyone who believes in him may have eternal life" (vv. 14–15).

This is the mystery of the cross. Colossians 2:15 says, "And having disarmed the powers and authorities, he made a public spectacle of them, triumphing over them by the cross." This is why, when we find John weeping in Revelation 5 because no one was found worthy to break the seal and open the scroll, the angel says to John, "Do not weep! There is one who is worthy, see the Lion of the tribe of Judah. He has triumphed and He is able to open the scroll and its seven seals" (v. 5, paraphrased). John looks up to see the Lion, and what does he see? He sees a lamb, looking as if it had been slain. You see, the power of the Lion is in the lamb. He is both sacrifice and deliverer!

What does this mean for us? This helps us see the gospel through a more missional lens. We are participants with God Himself in this grand plan to redeem the world. It is the church of Jesus Christ that stands between the central act of redemption and the fulfillment of God's promise to Abraham to bless all nations. We are to embody the good news of the gospel for a world that clings to a false narrative. Once you lose the grand narrative and the great stream of redemption, and the final hope to which we are all moving, we become tone-deaf when God summons us. The world seems to believe that this life is all that there is. The only final destiny the world has is retirement. Today, hope for a happy retirement has replaced the glorious final hope of everlasting life, communion with God, and reigning and ruling with the saints for eternity. The great tragedy of this world is that they live in a very small, thimble-sized universe.

We have the joy and privilege of proclaiming through word and deed that God is redeeming the world. But the church today has often lost sight of this mission of the church. We go to church for our own fulfillment, rather than engaging with God's great redemptive plan. Mission, after all, is what it means to be elected by God. Not so we can revel in our being saved, but rather that we have been elected to bring the gospel to the world. We have a great message: the Triune God is putting an end to sin. He will crush all wickedness and rebellion. Human trafficking will finally be overturned. Broken lives will be made whole. God will speak the final word. All injustice will be righted. Every tear will be wiped away. The glorious banquet will be served. The door of the Father's house will be flung open. Satan, the roaring lion, will be silenced. Death will be vanquished, the nations will be redeemed, and God will be all in all!

> *Moses, champion of deliverance from the bonds of slavery;*
> *Jesus breaks the greater master—from our sin we're now set free.*

CHAPTER 7

Moses: A Prophet Like unto Me

Deuteronomy 18:15–18; 34:10

We have seen Moses as deliverer, but now let's focus on his role as prophet. We often associate the prophetic stream with Elijah, Samuel, or a great prophet such as Isaiah. However, the Old Testament portrays Moses as the pattern, or model, for all subsequent prophets. That is why, at the death of Moses, Deuteronomy 34:10 says, "No prophet has ever risen in Israel like Moses, whom the LORD knew face to face." A prophet is differentiated from a priest in his basic orientation and role. A priest stands facing God, interceding for the people; a prophet stands facing the people, announcing God's word to them. Prayer is often viewed as a priestly function because we come before God and intercede on behalf of others. Preaching, on the other hand, is part of the prophetic office because a preacher faces the people and declares God's Word.

Moses is a powerful prophetic figure because he goes up the mountain and speaks with God face to face, then comes down and proclaims the word to the people. To fully understand the necessity of this role, recall the scene at Mount Sinai after the Israelites first came out of Egypt. For days ahead of time, the people had consecrated and purified themselves before God. Finally, the Lord's presence descended on Mount Sinai to deliver the Law. Exodus 19:16 says that thunder clapped and lightning flashed, smoke billowed from the mountain, and the earth began to tremble. The Israelites heard a loud trumpet blast, which they identified with angels, and a thick cloud settled around the whole mountain. According to Exodus 20:18–19, "When the people saw the thunder and lightning and heard the trumpet and saw the mountain in smoke, they trembled with fear. They stayed at a distance and said to Moses, 'Speak to us yourself and we will listen. But do not have God speak to us or we will die.'" That was the birth of the prophet. The full manifestation of God's glory and presence was so great that the Israelites knew they could not receive it and live. They pleaded with Moses that it was too much for them and asked him to mediate God's word so that they wouldn't be destroyed by coming into the unmediated presence of God.

So Moses established the office of the prophet to mediate God's word and His presence.

God Reveals and Conceals

Exodus 33:11 says that "the LORD would speak to Moses face to face, as one speaks to a friend." And yet, just a few verses later, in verse 20, God says to Moses, "You cannot see my face, for no one may see me and live." Martin Luther said that God simultaneously reveals Himself and conceals Himself. Revelation means that God has made Himself known in an act of self-disclosure, but God's fullness is so great, His attributes so infinite, His glory so profound, that men and women can never fully grasp, comprehend, or experience God's full presence. Moses comes as close as anyone in the Old Testament to beholding God face to face, as much as that is humanly possible. It was like seeing God's face through a veil, and even that caused Moses' face to glow and radiate the glory of God when he descended from the mountain (see Exodus 34:29).

In Deuteronomy 18:15–16, Moses says, "The LORD your God will raise up for you a prophet like me from among you, from your fellow Israelites. You must listen to him. For this is what you asked of the LORD your God at Horeb on the day of the assembly when you said, 'Let us not hear the voice of the LORD our God nor see this great fire anymore, or we will die.'" And so there grew in the Israelite community a great messianic expectation that Moses' prophetic office would one day be reconstituted. Once again, there would be a prophet like Moses who would speak to God face to face and bring the word of God to the people the way Moses did. He would be known as the Prophet and recognized by a reenactment of the miracle of the manna. This was the Jewish tradition, supported by Isaiah 25:6, as they continued to look for a new Moses who would lead the people.

This expectation is what lies behind the significance of the feeding of the five thousand, the miraculous multiplication of the bread. This is why the feeding of the five thousand is the only miracle of Jesus' public ministry which is recorded in all four Gospels: because, as a reenactment of the manna, it was considered essential to the telling of the gospel and the verification of the Messiah. When Jesus multiplies the loaves and feeds the people, their response is: "Surely this is the Prophet who is to come into the world" (John 6:14). Just as Moses prophesied, God sent a prophet like unto him. Jesus was born into Judaism, and was a prophet in the sense that He represented the veiled presence of God. As the second person of the Trinity, He shares in the full glory, dignity, majesty, and power of the Godhead, but He emptied Himself, took on human flesh, and stepped into human history. This is the role of the prophet: to mediate God's word, so we won't be destroyed as we would if we were brought into the unmediated presence of God. Moses had, more than anyone before or since him, seen the face of God—even if veiled. Jesus came from the very presence of the Father. In fact, Jesus is the incarnation (the very Word) of God Himself. To look into the face of Jesus is to see the face of God, veiled in human flesh, but revealing God's word and enabling us to know His commands.

And so we witness the true fulfillment of Moses' prophetic role in the person of Jesus Christ, the ultimate intermediary between a sinful humanity and a holy God. We are members of the human race. Not one of us can approach the consuming fire of God's holiness without being clothed in the robes of the great Prophet. Jesus is both the embodiment and the fulfillment of God's holiness. Just as Jesus is the tangible extension of God's holiness in the world, so we are to represent and embody His holiness in the world through our lives and our active witness in the world.

Moses spoke the Word of God through which we saw our need of grace;
Jesus, greatest Prophet, in You we behold God face to face.

CHAPTER 8

Christ, Our Lawgiver!

Deuteronomy 5:6–21; 18:15; Acts 3:17–26;
Matthew 5:17–20

What is our relationship to the Old Testament law? This is surely one of the great challenges we face as Christians on this side of the empty tomb. On the one hand, Paul in Romans 7:12 and 1 Timothy 1:8 says that the law is holy, righteous, and good. This is why the church throughout the centuries has continued to use the Ten Commandments as a cornerstone of Christian catechesis, along with the Lord's Prayer and the Apostles' Creed. On the other hand, Hebrews 8:13 says that the new covenant has made the old covenant obsolete and it will soon disappear. In Galatians 3:24–25 Paul indicates that the law was a tutor to lead us to Christ, but now that Christ has come, we are no longer under the supervision of the law. Paul says we have "died to the law" (Gal. 2:19), but he also says the "law is spiritual" (Rom. 7:14).

The unhappy resolution of this tension in many churches has been to distance Christians from the law and refer to the Old Testament as the covenant of works and the New Testament as the covenant of grace. This creates a separation of the two testaments and inadvertently denies the powerful theme of grace in the Old Testament as well as the ongoing role of the law in the New Testament. We lose the grand narrative of Scripture and we start asking the wrong questions, such as, which of the 613 burdensome laws of the Old Testament do I still have to carry?[2]

Christ Fulfills the Law

The purpose of this devotional is to better capture how Christ comes to fulfill, not abolish, the law; and to clarify how we relate to the law as those whose primary identity is being in Christ. We must begin by going back to one of the most important messianic prophecies given by Moses, which was explored in the previous chapter. Deuteronomy 18:15 said: "The LORD your God will raise up for you a prophet like me from among you, from your fellow Israelites. You must listen to him." This set into motion an expectation that the prophetic mantle of Moses would return and rest on the Messiah—and that He would be a new lawgiver.

The notion of Jesus as Lawgiver emerges in the Sermon on the Mount found in the gospel of Matthew (chapters 5–7). The parallels between Moses and Jesus are significant: both climb a mountain—Moses climbed Mount Sinai, and Jesus climbed a mountain to give the Sermon on the Mount. Moses gives the Law to the twelve tribes, Jesus to the twelve disciples. Listen to what Jesus says about the Law in the Sermon on the Mount:

> "Do not think that I have come to abolish the Law or the Prophets; I have not come to abolish them, but to fulfill them. For truly I tell you, until heaven and earth disappear, not the smallest letter, not the least stroke of a pen, will by any means disappear from the Law until everything is accomplished. Therefore, anyone who sets aside one of the least of these commands and teaches others accordingly will be called least in the kingdom of heaven, but whoever practices and teaches these commands will be called great in the kingdom of heaven. For I tell you that unless your righteousness surpasses that of the Pharisees and the teachers of the law, you will certainly not enter into the kingdom of heaven." (Matt. 5:17–20)

It is clear that Jesus fulfills the law of Moses perfectly. But let's take some time and carefully examine what Jesus does in His stature as the new Lawgiver. He begins by taking two of the Ten Commandments, which serve, I think, as representative of the whole table of the Law. In other words, Jesus could have gone through each one, but He chooses two to show us the way. Jesus, as the new Lawgiver, takes the sixth and seventh commandments: you shall not murder, and you shall not commit adultery. He says, "The Law says you shall not murder, but I say unto you, don't even be angry with your brother." Now, murder is an outward act done physically in the body. Anger is an inner disposition, which is not always manifested outwardly in a way that can be legally adjudicated. It is the same with the seventh commandment: do not commit adultery. This is an outward act done physically in the body in violation of the marriage covenant. Jesus, once again, moves from an outward act of the body to the inner disposition of the heart when he says, "But I tell you that anyone who looks at a woman lustfully has already committed adultery with her in his heart" (Matt. 5:28). He illustrates how in the kingdom these commands are not abolished, but actually deepened, from outward acts to inner heart dispositions. If you do not have lust in your heart, then a law that says you shall not commit adultery has no power over you! In that sense, and *only* in that sense, is the Law dead. If your heart has been redirected to the kingdom of God, then the Law loses its power. In fact, the book of Hebrews says that it is even obsolete. But it is not that the Law is abolished by being swallowed up in a sea of easy grace. The moral force of the Law is still very present, and actually deepened.

Jesus then moves from the formal Decalogue to the popular legal tradition of the Pharisees, which was prevalent in His time. He takes seven examples from their practice and demonstrates how the Pharisees had put fences up around the law that enabled them to keep the outward law but still have hearts that remained unchanged. He addresses (1) divorce, (2) oath taking, (3) retribution: eye for an eye and tooth for a tooth (*lax talionis*), (4) the Pharisees' interpretation of Leviticus 19:18: "Love your neighbor," (5) giving to the needy, (6) prayer, and (7) fasting. Again, Jesus demonstrates the inner motivation and heart behind these laws, and especially points out the way the pharisaical distortions had actually found ways to keep the letter but to defy the spirit of the law. Jesus exposes all of this, and in the process reveals a deep kingdom ethic as the new Lawgiver for the people of God.

Jesus challenges their hardened hearts, which give rise to easy divorce, and He restates God's original vision for marriage. He exposes the Pharisees' use of tiny technical distinctions in order to allow them to disobey the clear teaching of Scripture. Jesus takes their understanding of retribution (eye for an eye, tooth for a tooth) and calls us to turn the other cheek, to love our enemies, and to pray for those who persecute us. He challenges the idea of giving to the needy or fasting only to be seen by others rather than giving or fasting from pure motives. In all of these examples the clear message here is that in the kingdom we do not meet the abolition of the law in the sense of being freed from moral boundaries. Rather, the opposite. The law could only regulate outward behavior, whereas the law of Christ penetrates to the very core of our being, even down to the motivations of our hearts.

And so we witness the true fulfillment of Moses' prophetic role in the person of Jesus. Remember the last part of the prophecy, for when the prophet comes in Deuteronomy 18:15, "You must listen to him." When Jesus ascended another mountain in His transfiguration, the glory of God was revealed just as it had been on that terrifying day at Mount Horeb. Just as Moses, hidden in the cleft of the rock, was allowed to see God's back as He passed, so here, for just a moment, the curtain was pulled back, and the disciples were allowed to capture a glimpse of the glory of God. They saw the blinding light and heard the voice speak from heaven, "This is my Son, whom I love. *Listen to Him!*" (Mark 9:7, emphasis mine). There's that phrase from Moses' prophecy again. Jesus is God's great Prophet, the Second Moses, the New Lawgiver, sent down from heaven so that we may behold the glory of God. Listen to Him! All the prophets and all the prophecies of the Old Testament ultimately find their fulfillment in Jesus Christ. He is God's greatest prophet, bearing God's word. The difference is that Jesus does not just bring God's word like some messenger who arrives breathless with an important message in his or her hand, or even as Moses, who carried the Law down the mountain. Rather, Jesus *embodies* the Word of God—he is the Word made flesh. He is God's final Word to the human race. All subsequent words which are spoken, whether by preachers in pulpits, or the more informal witness of Christians, must resonate with and bear witness to that final Word, Jesus Christ. In Him, God's message and God's messenger fully meet.

The implication this has for our lives is profound. As the people of God, we are now joyfully under the law of Christ. Through the Holy Spirit we have been empowered and our hearts have been changed, so that we live under the new ethos of the kingdom, which deepens the law at every point. If they slap you on the face, turn the other cheek. If they demand your tunic, give them your cloak as well. If they ask you to go one mile, go two miles! This is about joy and freedom in Christ, not doubling up on the law's demands. The seventeenth-century writer and preacher John Bunyan, who wrote *Pilgrim's Progress*, also wrote a poem that summarizes beautifully what it means for Christ to fulfill the law. Bunyan wrote:

[To walk and to run] the Law commands,
but gives us neither feet nor hands.
Far better news the gospel brings:
it bids us fly and gives us wings!

In conclusion, we do not pit the law against grace. The law of God is always God's gift to us, whether it came on tablets of stone, or it is written by the Holy Spirit into our hearts.

That's what Wesley meant by being made perfect in love, or entire sanctification. It is love which sets us free—and that was always the intent of the law. There is only one grand story of redemption, and it spans both testaments!

There is no Sermon on the Mount if the law of God had not thundered on Mount Sinai! There is no Christ on a cross if the Red Sea had not parted! There would be no Eucharist if manna had not fallen in the wilderness! There is no church of Jesus Christ if there had been no temple in Jerusalem! There is no grace of God without the law of God, because law is an expression of God's grace, and grace has no meaning apart from the great moral framework of God's holiness.

Moses, giver of the law in which we see God's holy-love;
Jesus both fulfills the Law and calls us on to perfect love!

CHAPTER 9

Great David's Greater Son

2 Samuel 7:11b–16

We have seen Christ's fulfillment of the second Adam, the blessing and sacrifice of Abraham, and the Deliverer, Prophet, and Lawgiver of Moses. Now we turn our attention to His fulfillment of the kingship, as embodied in David. Looking back to 2 Samuel, we see that the origin of the kingship was not for the sake of seeing God's kingly rule visibly embodied among the Israelites; no, it was born out of rebellion and rejection of God's rule. Israel wanted a king because they wanted to be like all the other nations (see 1 Samuel 8:20). Samuel even told them to their faces that their demand for a king was a rejection of God's rule over them. When Samuel came before the Lord with their request, the Lord said, "Listen to all that the people are saying to you; it is not you they have rejected, but they have rejected me as their king" (1 Sam. 8:7).

The people kept demanding a king, and Samuel finally anointed Saul, a man from the tribe of Benjamin. If you go back to Genesis 49 and read Jacob's prophecy over each of his twelve children, you will remember that he said Benjamin was a ravenous wolf who devours his prey (see Genesis 49:27). Contrast that with his prophecy concerning Judah: "The scepter will not depart from Judah, nor the ruler's staff from beneath his feet" (Gen. 49:10). The scepter is the major symbol of a king—his authority, power, and rule. The tribe of Judah, not Benjamin, was ultimately destined by God to be the bearer of the kingship. Because the kingship began out of rebellion rather than obedience, however, the first king was specifically chosen from Benjamin. Samuel even described this first king as a ravenous wolf by using the word *take* five times in his warning: he will *take* your sons and daughters and make them his servants, he will *take* the best of your crops, he will *take* your grain, and so forth. Samuel described how this new king would not serve the people, but would plunder and devour them. Their response, however, was still "We want a king over us. Then we will be like all the other nations" (1 Sam. 8:19–20).

David Represents God's True Kingship

Throughout this overview of essential Old Testament characters, we have seen a number of important choices which the people of God had to make: Adam's choice to obey God's voice and submit to God's rule or to take of the fruit, assert his own rule, and try to be like God; Abraham's choice to follow in the pattern of the world, settle down, and make a name for himself, or to become a pilgrim for the Lord and let God make his name great; Moses' choice to attempt deliverance in his own strength or to wait on God to equip him. Likewise for Israel, Saul and David became symbols of two very different types. Saul is the anti-king, representing all the ways we assert our own rule over God's rule; David represents the true kingship of God's righteous rule and reign. Saul represents human strength; he was literally a head taller than any of the other men, handsome, physically strong, self-confident, and impressive to look at. David was the picture of human frailty; the youngest in his family, small, a child, and a shepherd. Saul trusted in his own strength rather than in God. He directly disobeyed God's command to destroy the Amalekites completely and kept some of their animals for a sacrifice. When he got impatient waiting for Samuel to come, he made the sacrifice himself in direct disobedience to the separation of kingly and priestly functions. David, by contrast, knew his own weakness and therefore trusted in the Lord. Saul did not have a repentant heart that was sensitive to the Lord's rebuke. Even after Samuel confronted him, he cared only for maintaining his image before the elders of Israel

(1 Sam. 15:30). David, meanwhile, was a man after God's own heart who, even in his sinful mistakes, was quick to repent and ask forgiveness.

When Samuel anoints David as king, we notice that he is from Bethlehem, of the tribe of Judah. He is chosen from among his seven older brothers, to the astonishment of his father, Jesse, and the prophet Samuel. Rejecting the tall, physically impressive sons, God reminds Samuel, "Do not consider his appearance or his height. . . . The LORD does not look at the things people look at. People look at the outward appearance, but the LORD looks at the heart" (1 Sam. 16:7). David is chosen for that heart which God desired and for that character which would set him apart as Israel's greatest king.

Early on, David's character is revealed in a way that dramatically contrasts with Saul. Saul was interested in settling down, making his own name great, and building his own kingdom. David, in contrast, when confronted by Goliath, revealed his trust in God's word and God's faithfulness. Throughout the encounter, he was more interested in God's honor and God's glory than his own name or honor. Remember that it took Moses forty years in the wilderness of Midian to learn that his greatest provision was God's name ("I Am" has sent you), God's authority (staff), and God's word (God gave him the words to speak). David, it seems, understood those basic lessons even as a young person. He declared to Goliath, "You come against me with sword and spear and javelin, but I come against you in the name of the LORD Almighty, the God of the armies of Israel, whom you have defied" (1 Sam. 17:45). David exemplifies one who trusts in God's name, God's authority, and God's word.

After David consolidated his rule over Israel, and the ark of the covenant was brought to Jerusalem, the Lord spoke to David, saying, "The LORD himself will establish a house for you: When your days are over and you rest with your ancestors, I will raise up your offspring to succeed you, your own flesh and blood, and I will establish his kingdom. . . . Your house and your kingdom will endure forever before me; your throne will be established forever" (2 Sam. 7:11b–12, 16). From this promise developed the messianic expectation that the Messiah would come from the tribe of Judah, and specifically from the line of David and the town of Bethlehem. This becomes part of Israel's hope, as demonstrated in texts such as Psalm 132:11, Micah 5:2, and Isaiah 9:6–7. Even in the midst of judgment and exile, when the lofty cedars of Lebanon were felled and the forests cut low, Isaiah reminded the people that a shoot would come up from the stump of Jesse. When Gabriel appears to Mary in Luke 1:32–33, he says of Jesus: "He will be great and will be called the Son of the Most High. The Lord God will give him the throne of his father David, and he will reign over Jacob's descendants forever; his kingdom will never end."

This is why one of the most important titles of Jesus in the New Testament is "Son of David." Jesus Christ is great David's greater Son. In Psalm 110, David even recognized that his son would be greater than he was by calling his son "Lord." David ruled an earthly throne; Jesus sits at the right hand of the Father. David won many earthly battles; Jesus won the cosmic battle against the powers of Satan. David was but a reflection of God's kingly rule; Jesus is the embodiment of the kingdom. David was a man after God's own heart; Jesus is the very heart of God Himself. Jesus is the perfect embodiment of the righteous rule and reign of God. Today, we can praise Him and proclaim Him King. We can declare that every knee shall bow and every tongue confess that Jesus Christ is Lord, to the glory of God the Father (Phil. 2:10–11)! We can prophetically see that one day, the kingdoms of this world will become the kingdom of our Lord and of His Christ, and He will reign forever and ever (Rev. 11:15). One of the great joys we have as Christians is that we can look in the back of the book and know who wins! We know the final outcome! Jesus is Lord. The Lion of the tribe of Judah rules and reigns over the universe. To Him who sits upon the throne and to the Lamb be praise and honor and glory and power forever and ever. Hallelujah!

David, royal king who led God's people to great vict'ries won;
Jesus, sovereign King of all kings—Hail, great David's greater Son!

CHAPTER 10

Christ, the Suffering Servant

Isaiah 42:1–9; 49:1–6; 50:2–9; 52:13—53:12

These devotionals have highlighted various streams that prefigure the coming of Jesus Christ. We see that Christ not only comes to earth as perfect man (the second Adam), but He also comes as our High Priest, our Prophet-Redeemer, our Final Sacrifice, our Lawgiver and our King. These prophetic, redemptive, priestly, and kingly streams all flow into the mighty rushing river of messianic expectations that reach their fulfillment in the Lord Jesus Christ.

Devout Jews would have all been familiar with these themes. Everyone knew that when the Messiah came, He would fulfill these expectations. However, we know from reading the New Testament that when the incarnation actually happened, it caught everyone by surprise. If Jesus had come forth like a mighty warrior and overthrown the power of Rome, many would have said that this was exactly the way they expected His kingly role to be fulfilled. What we discover, however, is that Jesus fulfilled these roles in ways that were unexpected. No one could have imagined that Jesus would come to suffer and die on the cross. It was completely scandalizing to think that this suffering Jesus was actually God in the flesh. There was no preparation to consider the possibility that God Himself would come to earth as the Great High Priest and then offer *Himself* as the sacrifice before rising again as the victorious King. Or was there? Throughout the pages of Israel's history, there was indeed a more subtle strand, a nuanced preparation for this unexpected revelation of Messiah that would only be understood in retrospect, as the early Christians looked back upon their own prophets' message. This is the surprise fifth figure of Christ as Suffering Servant.

Biblical References to the Suffering Servant

There are four passages in Isaiah that highlight this fifth major figure, which is mysteriously known simply as the Suffering Servant. These texts are found in Isaiah 42:1-9; 49:1-6; 50:2-9; and 52:13–53:12. There are several important themes that are found in these passages. First, the Suffering Servant is sent on a mission from God. Second, the mission involves suffering on behalf of another. Third, although the Servant will suffer and be rejected, he will, in the end, be exalted and vindicated. Finally, his suffering will bring justice, salvation, and blessing to all nations.

This devotional will focus on the fourth Suffering Servant song found in Isaiah 52:13–53:12. The song is preceded by a scene in heaven where God declares how beautiful are the feet of His messenger who will bring good news and announce salvation (Isa. 52:7). The servant is sent on a mission from God. God declares that "my servant shall prosper" (52:13 NRSV). He will receive a threefold blessing of being "raised and lifted up and highly exalted" (52:13). The language reflects the coronation and exaltation of a king being exalted in God's presence. However, this extraordinary exultation is set against the backdrop of suffering. As the passage continues, we see that He is "marred" and "disfigured" (52:14). He is "despised and rejected by men, a man of sorrows, and familiar with suffering" (53:3). The song goes on to declare that the Servant will suffer on behalf of another: "Surely he took up our infirmities and carried our sorrows" (53:4). "He was pierced for our transgressions, he was crushed for our iniquities; the punishment that brought us peace was upon him, and by his wounds we are healed" (53:5). It was the will of God that this Servant experience suffering, for it was through the vicarious suffering of the Servant that "my righteous servant will justify many" (53:11) and bear the sin of many, making intercession for the transgressors (53:12). The unfolding picture of the Servant is predicted to cause astonishment among the nations, and silence the kings of the earth (52:15).

The quotation of the Suffering Servant songs in the New Testament makes it clear that the early church understood that Jesus Christ was the Suffering Servant. He was sent on a mission from God that would involve suffering on behalf of others. It was only through that suffering that the nations would be redeemed and God's ultimate plan would be accomplished.

When Jesus came and began to heal the sick and cast out demons, the gospel of Matthew identifies Jesus with the Suffering Servant, who "took our infirmities and bore our diseases" (Matt. 8:17 NRSV, quoting Isa. 53:4). Later, after the resurrection, Philip encountered an Ethiopian eunuch in his chariot, reading the Suffering Servant song from Isaiah 53. The book of Acts specifically quotes the passage, which says, "Like a sheep he was led to the slaughter, and like a lamb silent before its shearer, so he does not open his mouth" (Acts 8:32 NRSV, quoting Isa. 53:7). We are told that Philip joined the Ethiopian in the chariot, and "starting with this Scripture, he proclaimed to him the good news about Jesus" (Acts 8:35 NRSV). The Ethiopian was baptized, becoming not only the first African Christian, but also signifying the global, multiethnic reach of the redemption found in Jesus Christ. The apostle Peter also identifies the Suffering Servant with Jesus when he declares about Jesus that "He committed no sin, and no deceit was found in his mouth" (1 Peter 2:22, quoting Isa. 53:9).

Jesus as Both Priest and Sacrifice

The earliest believers were totally disillusioned when Jesus was sentenced to die upon the cross. All of their messianic hopes seemed to be dashed to the ground. They did not see how Jesus' death could fulfill all of the kingly, prophetic, and priestly roles that they expected in their long-anticipated messiah. What they did not realize, however, is that there was a deeper plan that they had not anticipated: namely, that God would reveal his *greatest* glory through suffering. God would be exalted through humiliation. God would ultimately be victorious through apparent defeat. Christ would be both priest *and* sacrifice!

In C. S. Lewis's well-known story *The Lion, the Witch and the Wardrobe,* the evil witch demands the life of young Edmund, who had been revealed as a traitor. She demands exact and unmerciful payment. What he owes her must be paid and paid in full—with nothing less than Edmund's life. The great lion Aslan, who is the Christ-figure in the story, comes forward and tells the evil witch he will be willing to suffer and die in place of Edmund. The witch agrees and kills Aslan and celebrates her victory over her archenemy, the lion. However, at the dawn of a new day, Aslan rises from death to life. Aslan explains that although the wicked witch knew the "deep magic," which demanded the death of one who is a traitor, her knowledge only goes back to the dawn of time. Aslan knew a "deeper magic from before the dawn of time." That knowledge was that if a willing victim who had committed no treachery offered up his life for the traitor, then death itself would be overturned.

This is a picture of what God has done in the gospel of Jesus Christ. All of the great themes and figures in the Old Testament are brought together and fulfilled through the life and work of the Suffering Servant. Wesley summed up this amazing truth in his hymn "And Can It Be?"

> He left his father's throne above, so free, so infinite his grace,
> Emptied himself of all but love, and bled for Adam's
>   helpless race;
> 'Tis mercy all, immense and free, for O my God,
>   it found out me!
>
> 'Tis mercy all, the Immortal dies! Who can explore his
>   strange design?
> In vain the firstborn seraph tries to sound the depths
>   of love divine.
> 'Tis mercy all! Let earth adore, let angels minds
>   inquire no more!

The Suffering Servant Displays God's Love

The mystery of the Suffering Servant is, indeed, a strange design. Yet, this is what led the apostle Paul to declare that he determined "to know nothing while I was with you but Jesus Christ and him crucified" (1 Cor. 2:2). It is in the presence of the Crucified One, God's Suffering Servant, that we finally begin to see the full contours of God's great plan. In the gift of God's Son into the world—One born to suffer and die—we finally come to fully know and comprehend the love of God.

You may have been disappointed in the love you received from your parents, or, if you are married, from your spouse. However, in Jesus Christ the fullness of God's love is revealed. It is love alone that transforms us. We will never hate our sin enough to leave it. It is God's love that transforms us and empowers us to change. It is in the arms of His great embrace that we discover what it really means to be a child of God, adopted into His family. There are many wonderful things we can say about God. We can joyfully declare that our Triune God is a great King or our High Priest or the greatest Prophet, but there is no greater declaration than the profound truth that God is love, holy-love. Yes, God is love—we know it because Jesus Christ came into the world as the Suffering Servant. "For God so loved the world that he gave his only Son, so that everyone

who believes in Him shall not perish but have eternal life"
(John 3:16).

> *Prophets told of one whose suffering borne in love would end our pain;*
> *Jesus, perfect Suffering Servant, You have made us whole again.*
>
> *Jesus, Lord of all creation, Word of God in flesh made known;*
> *You have purchased our salvation—now our lives are Yours alone.*
> *Jesus, all our hopes fulfilling, second Adam, Abraham,*
> *Moses, David, Suffering Servant—God Himself, the great "I Am!"*

Christ, the Fulfillment

Tune options
BEECHER, NETTLETON, ODE TO JOY, STUTTGART, BEACH SPRING

Jesus, Lord of all creation, stepping into time and space;
Giving in your incarnation hope to all the human race.
Adam, as we share your nature, like you we stand bound
    in sin;
Jesus, now our second Adam—New creation you begin!

Abraham, a covenant was made with you by means of faith;
Jesus brings that faith's fulfillment, grafted in from every race.
Levi paid through Abraham a tithe unto the kingly priest;
Jesus, Most High Priest forever, interceding without cease.

In the sacrifice of Isaac, faith was proved and grace was found;
Jesus is God's sacrifice where grace and justice both abound.
Moses, champion of deliverance from the bonds of slavery;
Jesus breaks the greater master—from our sin we're now
    set free.

Moses spoke the Word of God through which we saw our
    need of grace;
Jesus, greatest prophet, in You we behold God face to face.
Moses, giver of the law in which we see God's holy-love;
Jesus both fulfills the Law and calls us on to perfect love.

David, royal king who led God's people to great vict'ries won;
Jesus, sovereign King of all kings—Hail, great David's greater
    Son!
Prophets told of one whose suffering borne in love would
    end our pain;
Jesus, perfect Suffering Servant, You have made us whole
    again.

Jesus, Lord of all creation, Word of God in flesh made known;
You have purchased our salvation—now our lives are yours
    alone.
Jesus, all our hopes fulfilling: second Adam, Abraham,
Moses, David, Suffering Servant, God Himself—the great
    "I Am!"

Notes

1. James LaGrand, *The Earliest Christian Mission to "All Nations": In the Light of Matthew's Gospel* (Atlanta: Scholar's Press, 1995), 180.

2. According to Jewish teachings, there are 613 laws in the Old Testament.

CPSIA information can be obtained
at www.ICGtesting.com
Printed in the USA
JSHW021018050520
5495JS00002B/7

9 781628 242423